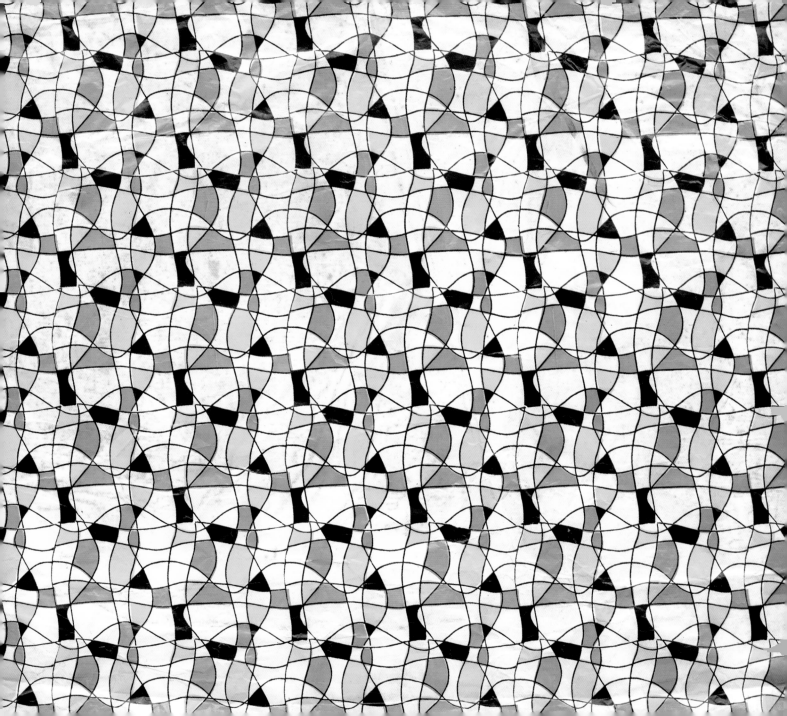

For Polly Alexander, as Granny would've wanted

First published in the United Kingdom in 2018 by
Pavilion
43 Great Ormond Street
London
WC1N 3HZ

ISBN: 978-1-911595-64-9

A CIP catalogue record for this book is available from the British Library.

10 9 8 7 6 5 4 3 2 1

Reproduction by Mission Productions, Hong Kong
Printed and bound by 1010 Printing International Ltd, China

This book can be ordered direct from the publisher at
www.pavilionbooks.com

GRANNY'S KITCHEN CUPBOARD

JOHN ALEXANDER

PAVILION

In *Granny's Kitchen Cupboard* you'll find a remarkable array of British mid-century household items and twentieth-century printed ephemera and packaging, as well as memorabilia from holidays abroad, all gathered by one woman, Jennifer Alexander. The contents reflect aspects of a long life; most of it lived in a single house in the Home Counties. None of these were brought together with the eye of a collector. Instead they were kept and reused in a way that says something about their time, in particular the thriftiness instilled by rationing in World War Two and after.

Paper bags from London department stores like Gamages, Lillywhites and Selfridges were put away for a rainy day. String was tidily wound and placed in a drawer. Tins that started out holding throat lozenges or Will's tobacco continued their useful life storing screws, nails and electrical fuses. For a lifetime, a Fortnum & Mason chocolate box held buttons and thread on a drawing room shelf, and wrapping paper for Christmas and birthday presents came back every year.

Jennifer was born in Worsley, Lancashire in the early 1920s. Her father, Cyril (Peter) Keitley, was a regular officer in the Manchester Regiment, an infantry unit in the British Army. He and his wife Joyce, also known as Billy, had two children: John and his younger sister, Jennifer. Her mother's family, the Gibsons, lived in London. Jennifer remembered how scared she was as a little girl taking the long staircase to bed in the dark Edwardian interior of her grandmother's tall terraced house in Warrington Crescent, Maida Vale. She was no doubt delighted to reach the top and be reunited with her extraordinary orange spotted cuddly dog and Pekingese pyjama case.

The peripatetic life of an army child had its plus sides. In the 1920s, Jennifer's father was stationed in Burma and India and, on Christmas Day 1929, the officers of the battalion clubbed together to buy her a baby donkey that she subsequently rode happily to school. Like most army children, when Jennifer was old enough, she came back to England to continue her education. Leaving behind the donkey and a menagerie of other pets, she was sent to a girls' boarding school in Bushey, Hertfordshire. Jennifer remembered sitting in her dormitory over Easter with, on one side, a supply of chocolate sent by her parents to cheer her up, and on the other, a big glass of water to stop herself from being sick from over-indulgence. The love of chocolate stayed with Jennifer throughout her long life.

Jennifer's brother John followed in his father's footsteps and went to Shrewsbury School at the same time as Richard Hillary, the fighter ace and author of *The Last Enemy*. John became a second lieutenant, also in the Manchester Regiment, and after the outbreak of World War Two father and son were both in France with the British Expeditionary Force. Sent back to rescue some men, John was killed on the retreat to Dunkirk in May 1940.

Jennifer herself served as a Third Officer in the Women's Royal Naval Service (abbreviated to WRNS, also known as the 'Wrens'). Founded in World War One as the women's branch of the Royal Navy, disbanded, and then revived in 1939, the Wrens were recruited under the slogan 'Join the Wrens and Free a Man for the Fleet' to fill a range of support and technical roles that, in World War Two, included flying transport planes. Jennifer was stationed on the east coast of Scotland at the Royal Naval Air Station at Arbroath, a training base for Navy pilots, and where Jennifer went through long checklists to make sure planes were ready for take off. Not a pilot herself, she did manage at least once to hop on a plane to London for the weekend. In September 1944, the Royal Duchess of Kent, the Commandant of the WRNS, visited the Arbroath station. In the photograph above, Jennifer can be seen in her uniform, in the back row, second from the right.

Douglas

After the war, Jennifer had two stints working at *The Queen* magazine. On a trip to Paris, perhaps with her mother, who was an accomplished watercolourist, Jennifer bought the small painting that became the cover of the December 1950 issue. Originally a high society magazine, at the end of the 1950s *The Queen* was bought by Jocelyn Stevens as a 25th birthday present to himself. He was later famous as a newspaper executive and chair of English Heritage. Renaming the magazine *Queen* and aiming it at a younger readership, Stevens appointed the cartoonist Mark Boxer as art director, and made the editor Beatrix Miller, who

went on to edit *Vogue* in the 1980s. Between them, they revolutionized magazines for women. In those days before air travel became unremarkable and Mediterranean beaches full of crowds, Jennifer and her mother holidayed in Norway and Spain. The hotel brochures, maps and itineraries in this book show an especially rich range of styles, reaching back to 1930s art deco and Scandinavian modernism. In 1960, Jennifer married and in the following year moved into the house in Surrey where the contents of *Granny's Kitchen Cupboard* were brought to light more than 50 years later.

KITCHEN CUPBOARD

SCALES

For many years, Salter Housewares produced Britain's best-selling brand of domestic weighing scales. In 1760, the brothers Richard and William Salter began making springs and pocket steelyards (spring balances) in a cottage in Bilston in the West Midlands of England. Nine years later, they established their company that produced the first spring scales in Britain. In 1825, their nephew George took over and renamed the company George Salter & Co. He produced a variety of housewares, including kitchen and bathroom scales, irons and mincers. The business thrived, and by 1950 it employed over 2,000 people. This Salter kitchen scale was made in 1957, manufactured in this chrome yellow as well as red, cobalt blue and aqua.

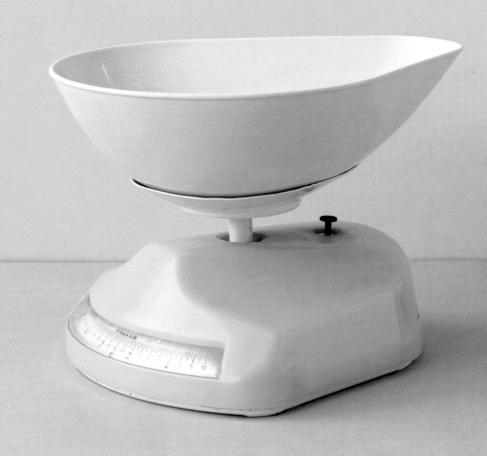

THERMOS FLASK

Invented by the chemist and physicist Sir James Dewar (1842–1923) in 1892 specifically to store chemicals at constant temperatures for experiments, the vacuum flask consists of two containers, one within the other, joined at the neck. They work by air being partially evacuated between the inner and outer vessels, creating a near vacuum. The Thermos flask was not manufactured for commercial use until 1904, when two German glass blowers formed Thermos GmbH. The name Thermos derives from the Greek word *therme* meaning 'heat'. In 1907, Thermos GmbH sold the rights to the Thermos trademark to three independent companies: The American Thermos Bottle Company in New York, USA, Thermos Limited in Tottenham, UK and Canadian Thermos Bottle Co. Ltd. in Montreal, Canada. In 1911, Thermos Limited of England produced the first machine-made glass filler. In 1923, this new large insulated food jar known as the Thermos Jumbo Jug was introduced and became instantly popular.

TEA AND RICE TINS

In 1899, Frederick Taylor and Thomas Law began a kitchenware manufacturing company. Combining their names, they created 'Tala' and it became one of Europe's most well-known kitchenware brands, producing such things as bread bins, spice racks, canisters and jelly moulds, as well as cleaning products and cake-making equipment. In the 1950s, the directors of Tala realised that post-World War Two housewives wanted bright modern accessories for their new labour-saving kitchens. Based on the cream and green tinware they had been producing already, they introduced their Matched Colourware in a range of bold colours. Catalogues showed their canisters, bread bins and cake tins as well as vegetable and toast racks, pedal bins and shoe-cleaning boxes. Colour combinations were red, blue, yellow and chrome combined with white or ivory.

TREATS AND CHOCOLATE

Fuller's and Bendicks are two confectionery companies
established in the late nineteenth and the early twentieth
centuries. Fuller's began in 1889, initially producing fudge,
peppermint lumps and walnut cake. By 1895, the founder
William Fuller had opened a factory in London's Wardour
Street along with his shops in Regent Street, Bayswater
and the Strand. The corporate red and white packaging was
introduced at that time. In 1920, Fuller's introduced their
own chocolates and in 1921, Rowntree took a controlling
interest of the company. By the 1950s, Fuller's had 82
shops and continued to expand and prosper, becoming
a favourite of many British families in the 1950s and
1960s. Bendicks is the combination of the names of Oscar
Benson and Colonel 'Bertie' Dickson, who began their small
confectionery business in 1930 at 164 Church Street in
Kensington, London. They made their first chocolates in a
tiny basement beneath the shop and became famous for
their unique chocolate 'bitter' mint recipe, made with almost
100% cocoa solids. The logo and lettering used on this
packaging dates from the 1970s. Dorlon of London, another
confectionery brand, was bought by Bendicks.

DORLON
victorian mints
STRONG MINTED CREAMS WITH SMOOTH DESSERT CHOCOLATE

FINEST
PRESERVED
GINGER

BY APPOINTMENT TO
H.M. QUEEN ELIZABETH II
ROBERT JACKSON & CO LTD
GROCERS

ROBERT JACKSON & CO. LTD

172 PICCADILLY W.1
01-493 1033

6a, 6b SLOANE STREET, S.W.1
01-235 9233

FORTNUM & MASON
PICCADILLY · LONDON W1

Fuller's
Crunchy
CHOCOLATE

BENDICKS
Bitter Mocha
FIRM COFFEE
FONDANT COATED WITH BITTER CHOCOLATE   200 g   7 oz Net Wt

BABY BURCO

Used for brewing, sterilising, washing and more, this Baby Burco was produced during the 1950s when the Burco Dean was formed through a merger of W. H. Dean (founded in 1895), producers of gas water heaters, and Burnley Components (Bur-Co), which produced electrical components. One of Burco Dean's first products was this 'Baby Burco' wash-boiler; produced originally for catering, it became popular for domestic use with an advertisement appearing in 1965 that stated in bold capitals: 'WHEN GERMS ARE ABOUT … EVERY WOMAN KNOWS BOILING IS THE ONLY SURE WAY TO KILL GERMS'. It became especially popular among housewives of the 1950s and 1960s for boil-washing terry towelling nappies.

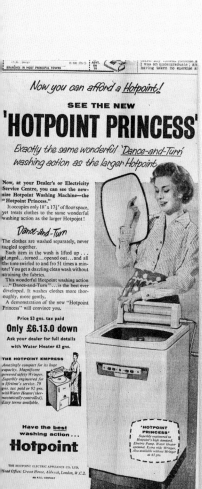

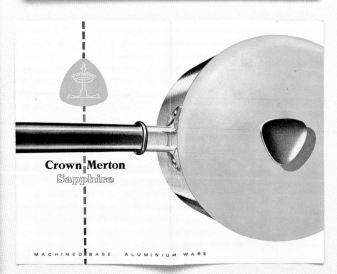

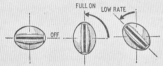

THE FLAVEL
RADFORD MK II HOTPLATE

This appliance is designed to comply with B.S.2491:1963
FOR USE WITH L.P. GAS
How to use this Appliance Economically

HOTPLATE

Both burners can be used for fast boiling or simmering and are controlled by safety taps of the self-locking type.

To turn on gas push in tap and turn in an anti-clockwise direction. The FULL ON rate is obtained when the tap is turned through 90° and a stop indicates when this has been reached. For the LOW rate position the tap should be turned a further 45°. However, if desired, the output of the burners can be set to any position other than the fixed LOW rate, by setting the control knob between LOW rate and FULL ON, or between FULL ON and OFF.

It is wasteful to use a saucepan less than 4 inches in diameter, as the flames will spread beyond the base of the saucepan. Make sure that the base of every kettle, saucepan or frying pan is smooth. Any roughness may damage the vitreous enamel of the hotplate.

GRILL (when supplied)

Whilst the grill is heating up, place the empty grill pan under the lighted burner to protect the enamel on the tray underneath. When the grill is red hot, place the loaded pan in the cooking position.

CLEANING

After use, whilst the hotplate is still just warm, wash with warm soapy water. If this is done regularly your hotplate will remain in good condition.

The enamel, when hot, should not be chilled with cold water. Spillage should be wiped off as soon as possible.

Do not use soda or caustic cleaning agents on any of the aluminium parts.

ADJUSTMENT

Your supplier will leave your Radford Mk. II Hotplate correctly fitted and adjusted, and should be informed immediately if any subsequent service is required. No one else should be allowed to interfere with your hotplate.

June, 1973.   D.4913/B
Sidney Flavel & Co., Leamington Spa.   P.T.O.

391
'ESTATE'
SERIES
COOKER

General Instructions

JACKSON

it's a
Russell Hobbs
Automatic Kettle

K3 Series
Instructions

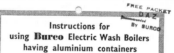

Instructions for
using **Burco** Electric Wash Boilers
having aluminium containers

FREE PACKET
Recommended
BY BURCO

GENERAL

The boiler container is made from aluminium which is anodised. The loading and voltage are as given on the serial number plate. The boiler MUST be used with a three pin socket and wired in accordance with the instructions attached to the cable. The socket capacity must be a minimum of 13 amps. The capacity of the container is specified on the serial number plate.

Non-Pump Models.

A rotary switch is fitted in a housing on the side of the boiler and is arranged to give either a three heat control, i.e. 'HIGH,' 'MEDIUM,' and 'LOW' heat with an 'OFF' position, or two heat control, i.e. 'HIGH' and 'LOW' with an 'OFF' position. In either application, when the water has boiled, 'LOW' heat maintains the water near boiling.

Pump Models.

In boilers fitted with a pump, the four position switch is marked 'HIGH,' 'LOW,' 'PUMP,' and 'OFF.' In use, the pump must only be used for emptying the container. It must not be used for circulating the water as an aid to washing.

IN USE

Care must be taken to ensure that water is present in the container before the boiler is switched on. Also it is essential that the boiler is switched off before all the water is drawn off from the container. Put sufficient water in the container to allow the clothes to move freely—water before clothes. NEVER PACK THE CLOTHES TIGHTLY. It is recommended for loading that 1 gallon of water be used for every 1 lb. of clothes. A typical working load for a 5¼ gallon boiler is approximately 4 gallons of water for 4 lbs. of clothes. Again, in a 10 gallon boiler approximately 7½ gallons of water are required for 7½ lbs. of clothes. Stir occasionally during heating. SODA MUST NOT BE USED WITH AN ALUMINIUM CONTAINER. The addition of bleach is NOT recommended, nor is the steeping of clothes. In order to keep the container in good condition, the use of a non-soap detergent, such as Daz, is recommended in preference to soap. If a soap powder, such as New Persil or Fairy Snow is used, DO NOT exceed the amount recommended by the manufacturer. In the course of time, the container walls may discolour; THIS IS NOT IN ANY WAY HARMFUL TO THE WASHING OF CLOTHES OR TO THE WATER, and is merely a chemical change of the surface of the aluminium.

AFTER USE

The pan must be cleaned with a wet cloth and fresh water. Washing residues soon harden on the sides and the bottom of the container and will, if not removed, not only cause clothes-marking but corrosion of the aluminium. Care must also be taken NOT to scour the pan, as this will damage the protective coating on the aluminium. For pump models, the drain hole from the container is covered by a filter which is clipped firmly into position, but which is readily removable. To maintain efficiency of the pump, this filter should be removed and cleaned after each wash and at least one gallon of clean water should be put into the container and then pumped out. Care should be taken to REPLACE the filter after cleaning.

CARE OF TAP

On boilers fitted with taps it is advisable to grease the tap threads every 3 months. To do this, open the tap until the small securing screw in the side of the tap body is accessible. Loosen the screw sufficiently to free the tap plug and unscrew and remove the plug. Brush the threads on the plug and then smear them very lightly with Wakefield Teservoor grease No. 3. Replace the tap plug and tighten the securing screw. Tubes of grease for this purpose may be obtained from the Burco Service Department at a small charge.

HARD WATER

Hard water causes clothes-marking and wastes soap. Hard water contains certain salts which react with soap, forming LIME SOAP SCUM. On heating, when approaching boiling point, this scum coagulates becoming a plastic substance, which on getting into clothes is most difficult to remove. The remedy is to use a reputable detergent which does not form scum, but if a soap powder is preferred it is necessary to use a water softener such as Calgon. In using a water softener DO NOT exceed the amount recommended by the manufacturer. In hard water areas, it is advisable to de-scale the boiler at regular intervals. To do this, use a 5% acetic acid solution and boil. The length of boiling is dependent on the scale thickness.

In any communication to the Manufacturers, reference should be made to the type of appliance and the serial number.

BURCO LTD., BURNLEY, LANCASHIRE, ENGLAND   Tel. Burnley 7241/4 (4 lines)

Pr. X3439/7

the **ONLY** dishwasher...

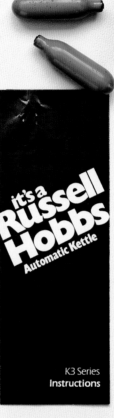

Hoover
Instructions for the use and care of the
JUNIOR CLEANER

YOUR **THERMOS** BRAND
VACUUM JAR

THERMOS

Sparklets
bulbs
TRADE MARK

morphy richards
Morphy Richards
Irons

APPLIANCE MANUALS

Hoover began as an American floor care manufacturer, established a base in the UK and, for the first half of the twentieth century, dominated the electric vacuum cleaner industry. The Hoover Junior, a small, upright vacuum, was introduced in the UK during the 1930s and soon became the biggest selling vacuum cleaner there.

Originally produced to create sparkling water for people living in the hottest locations of the British Empire, the Sparklets Soda Syphon was invented in the 1890s. Sparklets bulbs were also used during the Boer War. The Sparklets company stressed that their syphons were 'as easy for a housemaid in Bayswater' to use as 'for an orderly in South Africa'. In 1920, the British Oxygen Company took over Sparklets Ltd and by the 1970s, Sparklets Soda Syphons were de rigueur at any party.

IRON

Metal heating appliances, such as irons, toasters and electric fires, began to be produced for the domestic market in the 1930s, but at first they were exceptionally expensive. Seeing an opportunity, engineer Donal Morphy and salesman Charles Richards registered a private company manufacturing and selling electrical, gas, radio and television equipment in 1936. Its first product was a cheap electric fire and their next product, made in 1937, was an electric temperature-controlled iron that also sold for considerably less than competitors. By 1951, Morphy-Richards produced what it called the Atlantic Iron, which had a more ergonomic handle than their previous electric irons.

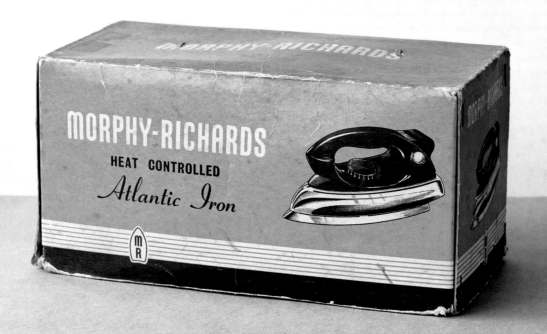

COOKING MANUALS

Robert Carrier (1923–2006) was an American chef, restaurateur and cookery writer who spent a large part of his career in England. In 1957, he began writing articles on food for *Harper's Bazaar*, *Vogue* and the *Sunday Times* colour supplement. In 1963, his articles were amalgamated to form a richly illustrated cookery book, *Great Dishes of the World*. In 1959, Carrier opened a restaurant in Islington, followed by a cook-shop in Harrods that grew into a chain. His recipes began to be printed on wipe-clean cards that became popular with housewives. In the late 1970s, he presented a television series called *Carrier's Kitchen*.

PORK **LAMB** **LAMB** **BEEF** **BEEF**

LEG

FMC

FMC

SHANK END

THICK FLANK

FILLET

TOPSIDE

KNUCKLE

CHUMP CHOP

CHUMP CHOP

LOIN

RUMP

FILLET

RUMP STEAK

SILVERSIDE

SCRAG END

SIRLOIN

ROLLED RIB

MIDDLE OF NECK

BEST END

LOIN CHOP

CHOP

BEST RIB

BRISKET

CHUCK

BREAST

SHOULDER

NECK

SHOULDER

SHIN

SHOULDER

ROBERT
CARRIER
COOKERY CARDS
Favourite Recipes I

MEAT
POULTRY
&
GAME

the Cooker.

boiling plates

The new fast boiling Speeding Plates or Radiant Plates are fitted to Jackson Cookers.

1 To keep the Speeding Plates in good condition and free from rust, smear occasionally with a little olive oil.

2 2, 3 or 4 pans can be kept boiling on one plate when necessary.

3 Boiling point will frequently be retained for some time after the Switch has been turned off from high.

boiler-grill or eye-level grill

Turn the control to "HIGH" for two or three minutes before toasting or grilling.
When the switch control is turned to "MEDIUM" the heat is reduced by half and when turned to "LOW" it is reduced to a quarter.
NOTE : When the Grill Boiler where fitted is not required for grilling it is more economical to use a Boiling Plate for boiling.

vegetable boiling

Use ½ pint of water to every one pound of vegetables. There is no necessity to use large amounts of water. Cook with the lid on.

egg boiling

Cover the bottom of the saucepan with water (about 2 tablespoonfuls). Place the eggs in the pan and replace the lid. Bring to boil on "FULL" (about 3—4 minutes). Turn the currents off and without raising the lid leave for three minutes, when the eggs will be cooked. When hard boiled eggs are required, four tablespoonfuls of water are necessary, and leave for 10 minutes.

ROBERT CARRIER COOKERY CARD
8 Saltimbocca all'Alfredo

ROBERT CARRIER COOKERY CARD
6 Blanquette de Veau

ROBERT CARRIER COOKERY CARD
5 Lamb Curry

...ant with Green Apples

ROBERT CARRIER COOKERY CARD
9 Cold Parsleyed Ham

ROBERT CARRIER COOKERY CARD
7 Vitello Tonnato

WOMAN'S JOURNAL
THE PERFECT OMELETTE BO...

RECIPES

During the 1960s and 1970s, food photography followed
certain accepted rules. Always shot from slightly above,
a lot of food was first coated with glycerine to make it
shine under the bright lights, or sprayed with hairspray to
give it a healthy-looking bloom. Boldly coloured plates and
tablecloths were used to make everything look appealing.
But the food itself was often not what it seemed. For
instance, mashed potato or shaving foam was substituted
for ice cream or cream, as hot studio lamps would melt the
real thing. Photographs were retouched to make everything
more colourful, but by the late 1970s, new types of printing
methods from Japan gave the colours greater clarity.

Coq-au-vin à la Beaujolaise

8 *Saltimbocca all'Alfredo*

7 *Vitello Tonnato*

5 *Lamb Curry*

6 *Blanquette de Veau*

Old English Chicken Pie

9 *Cold Parsleyed Ham*

10 *Ham and Mushroom Pancakes*

11 *Cotechino Sausage with Lentils*

20 *Pigeons Confits aux Raisins*

Pheasant with Green Apples

17 *Duck and Orange Salad*

16 *Duck with Sauerkraut and Apple Stuffing*

19 *Game Pie*

12 *Roast Chicken with Watercress Stuffing*

MEDICINE CABINET AND COSMETICS

TINS

From the early nineteenth century, patented medicines
and related products were often packaged and sold in tins.
Victorian and Edwardian packaging was frequently quite
wordy and flowery. Curly banners, serif fonts and over-
enthusiastic claims of a product's efficacy all gradually
became replaced by greater clarity and integrity. As many
of these tins date from the 1950s, 60s and 70s, they
display the later twentieth century's aim to appear honest,
dependable and eye-catching, but not too exuberant
or ornate.

Since 1958, Strepsils throat lozenges have been used to
relieve the discomfort of mouth and throat infections. Both
tins of Adexolin, which were vitamin C and D supplements,
were made after 1957. The tin of Compound Glycerin of
Thymol Pastilles with AMC dates from the 1960s, and this
version of Allenbury's Pastilles was sold in the 1950s. A
mild antiseptic, TCP is produced in France by Laboratoires
Chemineau and has been sold in Britain since 1918. Called
after its original chemical name, it is one of the most well-
known brands of antiseptic in the UK.

MEDICINE BOTTLES AND OINTMENTS

Gripe water was first developed in 1851 in England, and given to babies to ease the pain of colic. The formula contained sodium bicarbonate, alcohol, dill oil, water and sugar, and it was extremely popular with mothers until 1982, when it was banned for its alcoholic content. Other formulations have been produced without alcohol, but in general, the product has lost the popularity it enjoyed during the mid-twentieth century.

Sal volatile, also called smelling salts, ammonia inhalants or spirit of hartshorn, has been used since the Roman era to revive and restore. Mentioned in the writings of Pliny as 'Hammoniacus Sal' and in Chaucer's fourteenth century *Canterbury Tales* as 'Sal Armonyak,' smelling salts have a long history. During the nineteenth century, they were often dissolved in perfume, vinegar or alcohol and used to revive women who frequently fainted from over-tight corsets. During World War Two, the British Red Cross and St John Ambulance advised all workplaces to keep smelling salts in their first aid boxes, and many homes kept a bottle or two for the same reason.

MORPHINE

The commercial manufacture of morphine, first isolated by Friedrich Serturner in 1804, began in Germany in 1827. It was used throughout the American Civil War, World War One and World War Two as a powerful painkiller, even though its addictive properties were discovered soon after the American Civil War. Despite this, for many years it was available without prescription.

OTHER MEDICINES

Tan oil (with no sun protection factor), toothpicks, plasters and cotton buds are all basics of the 1950s and 1960s medicine cabinet. For centuries, poisonous plants such as belladonna and *Mandragora* have been used in poultices and salves for pain relief, as muscle relaxants and for their anti-inflammatory properties. The belladonna plaster was invented in the late nineteenth century, using the pulped foliage of the deadly nightshade plant. When this turned into liquid, it was soaked into cloth, and suspended there with oils and fats. When applied to a wound or against an area of pain, the bandage helped to ease discomfort. Soon belladonna plasters were produced with adhesive already applied so they adhered to the skin.

1 Only
12.5 x 19cm

POISON

BELLADONNA
HESIVE PLASTER B.P.

(PERFORATED) WHITE CLOTH

MANUFACTURED BY
EDWARD TAYLOR PLC
MONTON ECCLES MANCHESTER

Made in England

20

24P

Johnsons
cotton
buds

Flexible stems

Soft, gentle tips

KAYBEE 8
FLAT STYLE   GENRE PLAT

tooth
picks

CONTENTS 650

PORTIA

button end
Ref. 2139
Improved Moorfield glass medicine dropper

Made in England

B.P.C.
ABSORBENT GAUZE

one yard   STERILISED

CONFORMS WITH B.P.C. & N.H.S. SPECIFICATIONS

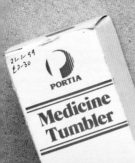

21-7-89
£2-30

PORTIA

Medicine
Tumbler

INNOXA

tan

OIL

TANS
PROTECTS
REPELS INSECTS

TANS PROTECTS REPELS INSECTS

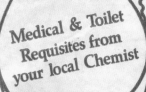

Medical & Toilet
Requisites from
your local Chemist

EYE CARE

In 1929, Dr Harry Benjamin published *Better Sight Without Glasses*, which has since, allegedly, helped thousands to improve their eyesight naturally. The book has become something of a cult, featuring eye exercises, advice on diet and relaxation that are claimed to eliminate or reduce the need for glasses. The book combines a naturopathic approach to health with an eye-training system devised by Dr William Horatio Bates, who was one of the best eye doctors in New York in the late nineteenth century.

PERFUMES AND SCENTED TALC

Often called 'the first couturier', Charles Frederick Worth (1825–95) dominated Parisian fashion after moving there in 1845 from Lincolnshire in England. He became internationally renowned for his innovations in couture and the House of Worth was also one of the first fashion houses to produce perfume. Les Parfums Worth used the latest technology and Je Reviens was its first fragrance; the result of a collaboration between Charles Frederick Worth's grandson Jacques and the perfumer Maurice Blanchet. During the 1950s to 1970s, Je Reviens became a classic, worn by film stars, aristocracy and 'ordinary' women everywhere.

TOILETRIES AND GROOMING

During the mid to late twentieth century, grooming products were fairly minimal. Most households had a styptic pencil; a medicated stick made of powdered alum crystal moulded together with a wax binder into a lipstick shape and size. Before the multi-blade razor was invented, styptic pencils sealed small cuts and nicks caused during shaving and so they were an essential part of most men's shaving kits.

During the 1860s, engineer and inventor Mason Pearson moved to London from Yorkshire and joined a partnership, later known as Raper Pearson and Gill, which made brushes by hand. Pearson invented a mechanical brush-boring machine, and soon after also designed the innovative rubber-cushion hairbrush, still used today.

MASON PEARSON
London. Eng.
HAIR BRUSH

Acetone

A useful solvent for various household purposes.

NOT TO BE TAKEN
HIGHLY INFLAMMABLE

Keep away from heat, naked flame and sparks.

Avoid inhaling the vapour and prolonged contact with the skin.

KEEP OUT OF THE REACH OF CHILDREN.

BOOTS PURE DRUG CO. LTD. NOTTINGHAM-ENGLAND

POWDER
LEICHNER
LONDON

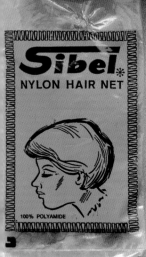

Sibel
NYLON HAIR NET

100% POLYAMIDE

ROUGE
DE THEATRE
BOURJOIS PARIS
FRANCE

STYPTIC
PENCIL

Boots
for men

STYPTIC PENCIL
ALUMINIUM SULPHATE B.P.C.

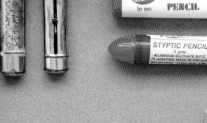

6

Now!

You can shave more
* naturally-
* closer, smoother
than ever before!

THE NEW
"NATURAL ANGLE"
RAZOR GLIDES
NEAR-VERTICALLY
DOWN YOUR FACE!

The weight is correct

The balance is correct

OLD WAY

*It's here! Ever-Ready's new "Natural Angle" Razor! New "Flat-top" design means the razor-head lies flat against the face, so the blade glides through your stubble at the natural, new vertical angle of 15°.

It shaves closer. Your finger-tips tell you your face is smoother.

The moment you take this new razor into your hand you know you've got a far more efficient shaving instrument.

Feel it. The balance is correct. The weight is correct.

See how fast it loads! Click it open ... insert the blade ... snap shut.

And how it saves! Blades last far longer because there's less wear on the cutting edge when the blade meets the stubble at the natural angle!

LIFE-TIME GUARANTEE! Every "Natural Angle" Razor carries a life-time guarantee of free service or replacement.

For a smoother face every day—shave the "Natural Angle" way—it's the new way to avoid 5 o'clock shadow.

Natural-Angle
Ever Ready
Razor

7/6

MERKUR

Solingen

MADE IN W. GERMANY

CUTEX
0
COLOURLESS

Royal Blade EverReady

Royal Blade EverReady

Royal Blade EverReady

THIS YEAR
I'm "plugging" for Leisure

**HOOVER &
ELECTROLUX** etc

(REBUILT)

FOR QUICKER, EASIER CLEANING

99/6
OF EASY TERMS

NO P.TAX

Limited quantity of Rebuilt and New cleaners at amazing low prices. New cleaners also available.

GENEROUS PART-EXCHANGE ALLOWANCES

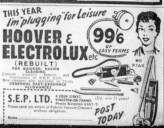

S.E.P. LTD. 4 EDEN STREET, KINGSTON-ON-THAMES
Phone Kingston 6661/2 (Est. over 25 years)

Please send me details of Rebuilt Vacuum Cleaners without obligation.

Name

POST
TODAY

SMOKING ROOM

CIGARETTES

In 1949 in Britain, it was estimated that 81% of men and 39% of women smoked. People smoked in their homes, cars, as well as in pubs, restaurants, hotels, shops and cinemas. Most homes had a selection of ashtrays and cigarettes, cigars and sometimes even pipes and tobacco to offer guests. King-sized, tipped, menthol and Turkish were just a few of the cigarette varieties available. With the introduction of ITV commercial television in 1955, cigarette companies brought the 'benefits' of smoking into homes. When it was introduced in the 1960s, Player's No. 6 became one of the bestselling brands.

Also known as the 'silent salesman', packaging is used to promote products, heighten their appeal and encourage purchase. Since World War Two, packaging design has become a huge business and was something that particularly preoccupied Pop artists in the 1950s and 1960s, at the time when many products were first pre-packaged, rather than being weighed and wrapped by shopkeepers. During the 1960s, advances in printing, and more time spent on typography and graphic design, meant that packaging became increasingly sophisticated.

Cigarettes have long been part of the consumer culture and were first packaged and marketed as being health-giving ('To keep a slender figure no one can deny, reach for a Lucky instead of a sweet' announced a highly successful ad in 1929 for Lucky Strike cigarettes). Brands like Lucky Strike ran several lucrative advertising campaigns featuring its packaging along with slender, healthy-looking young women and men to show that all the most attractive people smoked them. As more evidence has shown the dangerous effects of cigarette smoking, all cigarette packaging in the UK now has to be plain with no pictures or promotions, and to feature bold warnings stating that smoking the contents will harm children and cause cancer, amputation or death.

ROUGH CUT
FINEST SELECTED TOBACCO

SENIOR SERVICE
Cadets
FILTER VIRGINIA

Marcovitch
Black & White
Cigarettes
Made in London, England by
Marcovitch - Piccadilly W

SULLIVAN POWELL
BURLINGTON ARCADE. LONDON
THE BURLINGTON ARCADE
Special No1 Turkish
FILTER CIGARETTES

DUNHILL
LUXURIOUS TOBACCO
THE
Royal Yacht
MIXTURE
UNIQUE MIXTURE
INGLY MILD WITH A GRAND RICH
OUR - VERY SOFT SMOKING
BLENDED BY
ALFRED DUNHILL
LONDON
CTURED IN GREAT BRITAIN

SULLIVAN POWELL
BURLINGTON ARCADE LONDON
THE BURLINGTON ARCADE
Special No1 Turkish
FILTER CIGARETTES

SENIOR SERVICE
Cadets
FILTER VIRGINIA

BY APPOINTMENT TO
HER MAJESTY THE QUEEN
TOBACCONISTS
BENSON & HEDGES LTD
LONDON W1
BENSON and HEDGES
SUPER VIRGINIA CIGARETTE

BY APPOINTMENT TO
HER MAJESTY THE QUEEN
TOBACCONISTS
BENSON & HEDGES LTD
BENSON and HEDGES
SUPER VIRGINIA CIGARETTE
BLENDED WITH OTHER FINE TOBACCOS
Specially selected and packed for
BRITISH EUROPEAN AIRWAYS

YER'S
No6
FINEST VIRGINIA
TER

SULLIVAN POWELL
BURLINGTON ARCADE. LONDON
THE BURLINGTON ARCADE
Special No1 Turkish
FILTER CIGARETTES

MURRAYS
ERINMORE
MIXTURE
PIPE TOBACCO
NET WT. 50 g

CIGAR BOXES

During the Cold War, early in 1962, US President John F. Kennedy set up a trade ban as a move against Fidel Castro's Communist regime, which had seized control of Cuba in 1959 and then began confiscating private property and assets, including cigar companies. Included in the ban were the highly sought after Havana cigars. In October that year, Castro allowed the Soviets to build missile bases on Cuba that would be capable of striking the United States. To prevent Soviet ships from delivering the materials for the missile bases, America blockaded Cuba. Fifty-two years later, after Fidel Castro's death in 2016, the trade embargo was finally lifted.

PIPE TOBACCO

Traditionally used as a social or ceremonial tool, pipe smoking began among several ancient cultures and did not arrive in Europe until the sixteenth century. As well as tobacco and herbs, other substances have been smoked, including opium and various other addictive substances.

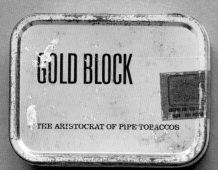

GOLD BLOCK

THE ARISTOCRAT OF PIPE TOBACCOS

WILL'S
CUT
GOLDEN BAR

DOUBLE THICK QUALITY
For cleaning stem of bowl.
Use Standard Quality for
mouthpieces.

JOHN SINCLAIR'S
Barneys
Empire Blend

WILLS
CUT
GOLDEN
BAR

READY RUBBED

A GOOD PIPE DESERVES CARE . . .
CLEAN YOUR PIPE REGULARLY!

1. FOR HYGIENIC REASONS - Care for your health
2. FOR A SMOOTHER, MORE SATISFYING SMOKE - A clean pipe smokes sweet
3. FOR LONGER PIPE...

THE BALKAN SOBRANIE

SMOKING MIXTURE

MATCHBOXES

The word 'phillumeny' derives from the Greek word *phil-* meaning 'loving' and the Latin word *lumen-* meaning 'light'. It was first used by the British collector Marjorie S. Evans in 1943 to describe a person who collects matchboxes, matchbox labels, match books and match-covers, which was becoming something of a worldwide phenomenon.

GITANES
BOUT FILTRE

DALLAS

AVERAGE CONTENTS 52 MATCHES
THE BLUE CROSS
SAFETY 3D MATCH
MADE IN NORWAY.
NITEDALS MATCH Co Ltd LONDON

TWA

Embassy
the best in smoking

MADE IN ENGLAND BY BRYANT & MAY LONDON

THE SHIP
SAFETY MATCH
BY JOHN MASTERS & Co LONDON

marquee
90 WARDOUR ST   01-437 6603
LICENSED BARS AND HOT FOOD
LIVE MUSIC — 7 NIGHTS A WEEK
AUSTRIAN MATCHES

SINCLETON & COLE
HYGIENIC
TINS OR PACKETS

SNUFF

IN NATIONAL
DEMAND

DINGWALLS
RHYTHM 'N' BOOZE

USE
RONSONOL
WORLD'S GREATEST
LIGHTER FUEL

AVERAGE CONTENTS 52 MATCHES
THE BLUE CROSS
SAFETY 3D MATCH
MADE IN NORWAY.
NITEDALS MATCH Co Ltd LONDON

CANDLES AND FUEL

During the twentieth century, power cuts for various reasons were not uncommon in many parts of the world, but during the early 1970s in Britain, the Three-Day Week was introduced. This scheduled power cuts across the country to conserve electricity because of industrial action by coal miners. From 1 January until 7 March 1974, commercial use of electricity was limited to three specified consecutive days' consumption each week. Essential services were exempt but television companies had to stop broadcasting at 10.30pm. In preparation for the blackouts, every household stocked up on a variety of candles and tapers.

CARS

The Morris Oxford advertisement is from October 1952, advertising the newly designed grille. Along with the Morris Minor, the Oxford became highly sought after.

In June 1905, in London's Trocadero restaurant, the British Automobile Association (AA) was created. It was a club for car enthusiasts that provided information about driving laws and car makes and models, and sold accessible road maps. Since then, the AA has grown to provide many more benefits including driving instruction, breakdown assistance and advice-filled handbooks. By 1939, nearly 35% of all UK drivers were AA members. Every member received a badge like this to screw on to his or her car radiator grille. In 1912, the first AA telephone boxes were erected and within eight years there were 61 across the UK. Each member was given a special key to open them and could use the telephones if they needed assistance.

every car
and
motor-cycle
in
Gt. Britain
needs

Punctureprufe

AA

Service for today's motorist

MSP 46 (1/3)

Get to know this magnificent Morris Oxford.
Experience the delight of its smooth-riding and
controllability, made possible by torsion-bar
suspension. Sense the feeling of spirited power when
the highway invites speed. Then examine it for
finish and styling. You'll discover it has "Quality
First" in all its features. Ownership will prove
that traditional Morris reliability is an
investment in long-lasting value.

You'll be glad you bought a

'QUALITY FIRST'

MORRIS *Oxford*

MORRIS MINOR • MORRIS OXFORD • MO

Morris Motors Limited, Cowley, Oxford. Overseas Business: Nuffield Exports Limited, Oxford

THE QUEEN, MARCH 25, 1953

fling
THE WAX'N SHINE
CAR SHAMPOO

AAH 484242   AAH 484242   AAH 484242

MONTH 6   MONTH 5   MONTH 4

ONE **S** UNIT

AAH 484242   AAH 484242   AAH 484242

MONTH 6   MONTH 5   MONTH 4

ONE **S** UNIT

WORLD WIDE
HERTZ
RENT A CAR

LONDON
Rate
SCHEDULE

Effective: May 14th, 1965
to October 18th, 1965

SHELL

MAP-POCKET COMPUTOR

27 16.8	60 37.3	4,000 2485.5

KILOMETRES TO MILES
YOU'RE NEVER FAR FROM

SUPER SHELL

NH4776812   NH4776812

Motor Fuel Ration Book

MOTOR CAR
1501 – 2200
C.C.

14 – 19
H.P.

The coupons in this book authorise the furnishing
and acquisition of the number of units of motor
fuel specified in the coupons.

SILVERWARE

Stainless steel cutlery, aluminium pans and silverware, such
as candlesticks, teaspoons and napkin rings, were common
in British homes in the 1940s, 50s and 60s, and specialist
metal cleaners and polishes were essential in many
everyday homes.

JACOBEAN

Goddard's
Plate Powder
1/-
The best polish for Silver...

Guarantee
and
instructions
on the care of
Aluminium
Ware

Here's how to make it last a lifetime...

Kindly recommend to your Friends, giving them our address.

PROF. THOMSON'S WONDERFUL DISCOVERY

The "MARVEL
MAGNET PLATE"

A QUICK, SAFE and EASY way of
Cleaning Gold, Silver, Platinum,
Diamonds, E.P.N.S., Glassware and
Electro Plate. It is:

Non-poisonous, non-injurious and will
not scratch as there is no friction.

DIRECTIONS FOR USE.

Water should be hot, but not boiling. Use Enamel or
Porcelain Basins only. Add four to five tablespoonsful of
Common Washing Soda to every quart of water. Place
the plate into the Soda Water, and then the articles on to
the plate, making sure the articles are completely covered.
Thoroughly rinse articles in Cold Water before drying.
Clean and dry the Plate. The Plate must not be in the
water whilst it is being heated. (Please read important leaflet inside.)

DO NOT USE METAL BASINS.

Prof. Thomson's 'MAGNET PLATE'
Only obtained from

THE SPRING SILENCER COMPANY,

Price 1/6   1 & 2, Hainault Road,
POST FREE   CHIGWELL, ESSEX.

LARGER SIZE OBTAINABLE

BEWARE OF IMITATIONS   ACCEPT ONLY PROF. THOMSON'S

PRICE 3/6
POST FREE.

B&H

STAINLESS
STEEL
TABLE
CUTLERY
CORPORATE MARK
GRANTED 1795

Boswell
Hatfield
& Co. Ltd.

SHEFFIELD
ENGLAND

Goddard's

Silver Dip
CLEANS SILVER SAFELY

"WARDONIA"
REGD
CELEBRATED

STAINLESS
CUTLERY

WARRANTED QUALITY
BEST SHEFFIELD
MANUFACTURE

Firths'
Stainless Steel
EXCLUSIVELY USED

SUPPLIED BY:-
SPRING SILENCER Co.
1 & 2, HAINAULT Rd.
CHIGWELL,
ESSEX.

HEATER

The HMV Cavendish Fan Heater was first manufactured by the Gramophone Company Ltd in England in 1949. From the early 1950s, it was advertised as being conveniently portable and able to warm an entire room through a fan that circulated the warm air. The red-tinted lamp created a warm glow, and the heater itself, made of Bakelite and pressed steel, was available in a range of colour combinations, including French grey with blue and cream with purple-brown. Because of the D-shaped body with semi-circular front, split into horizontal louvres, it became affectionately nicknamed 'the Beehive.'

MISCELLANY

Extracted from flax seeds, linseed oil has been used as a
preservative for wood and concrete, as well as an ingredient
in paints, varnishes and stains, for years. It is also used
traditionally for oiling cricket bats. First introduced in
1931, the His Master's Voice Portable Gramophone Model
102 was HMV's most successful and enduring portable
gramophone, sold until 1960, and marketed by HMV as
'THE WORLD'S FINEST PORTABLE.' Unique and versatile,
metallic paste known as Goldfinger was produced by
Rowney before it became Daler-Rowney in 1983, and is
still produced.

Rowney

Goldfinger

Rub on metallic finish
Buffs up to a fine lustre
Superbe lustre métallique obtenu
Après application et polissage
Metallpaste zum Verzieren
Poliere bringt einen feinen Glanz
hervor

22 ml

FOR INTERIOR & EXTERIOR USE

VALSPAR
2-4 Hour
LACQUER

BLACK

araldite hardener
araldite adhesive

ARALDITE

adhesive for china glass
metal rubber wood

and most materials in common use

Eclipse

**POCKET
MAGNET**

"HIS MASTER'S VOICE"
Portable Gramophone
MODEL 102

Instructions for Assembling and Operating

A. Issue 1.   Part No. 8776.

"Belling"

Zephyr
Convector

**Instructions for installing
and operating**

PORTABLE AND WALL FIXING MODELS
for use on AC only

SONY

TYPE II (HIGH) POSITION 90 MINUTES (45 MIN. EACH SIDE)

Metal Tape

METALLIC 90

135m COMPACT CASSETTE CASSETTE COMPACTE
TYPE IV METAL POSITION

SEALS · MAKES
MENDS · PACKS

UNWIND FROM
APPROX. 14 METRES

GUMST
SEALING

IS TWIGGY-
, ULTRA-SLIM,
BTRUSIVE
AK ELECTRIC
GE RADIATOR.

4" actual width . . .

2   3   4

SIGNPOST

RAW
**LINSEED
OIL**
Ref. 911

Packed by
Langston·Jones
& Samuel Smith Ltd.
Compton Works, Watts Grove
Bow, London, E.3
Telephone: EAST 3031

ORIS

REX
cold water
size

*for preparing
walls and ceilings etc.*

another REX product

BRITISH MADE

Brown's
"VICK"

**SEMAPHORE
CARDS**

Self-Examination
Self-Instruction

£2·00

Brown, Son & Ferguson, Ltd.
4-10 Darnley Street, Glasgow G41 2SD

Made and Printed in Great Britain

**YOUR
GUARANTEE**

WE
NEVER
FORGET
YOU

**SHOP
ELECTRIC**

TRAVEL TRUNK

How to pack your REV-ROBE

Start by opening your Rev-Robe. Detach the tray lid and hang up the Rev-Robe by the ring on the back. Unfasten the cross-strap; detach the metal 'crook' and let it hang down.

Your Rev-Robe is now quite ready for packing !

Specially designed hangers are included with this Rev-Robe.

Extra hangers may be purchased from your dealer if required.

1   2   3

1 Place your dresses on the hangers and hook the hangers on to the two side brackets at the top of the case. Be sure to hang the shorter dresses between the longer ones.

2 When you have finished hanging your dresses in the case, place the metal "crook" behind the skirts of the dresses, and . . .

3 . . . raise the crook, *holding the dresses firmly against it with your thumbs and forefingers to prevent the dresses slipping.* Place the ends of the crook on to the brackets at the top of the case. Fasten the cross-strap, lift Rev-Robe down, and lay it flat; dresses will settle comfortably into their compartment. Now replace lid,* making sure that the hinge projections are fully engaged in the corresponding slots on the body.

PACKING HINTS

No tissue paper is needed. Dresses which have travelled in a Rev-Robe can be worn immediately after unpacking —there is no pressing out to be done.

For coats and skirts : loop tapes of skirts on the notches of the hangers and hang the coats and skirts in between the dresses.

*TRAY LID MODELS

Pack shoes, underwear, etc., in the detachable tray-lid, placing the shoes at the end farthest from the lock hasps.

SUITCASE

Before the late nineteenth century, trunks were heavy, cumbersome and waterproofed for travelling on steamships. By the turn of the twentieth century, cases were being made as portable wardrobes. By the 1950s, with the wider availability of consumer air travel, suitcases became lighter and more convenient, with the new consideration of excess baggage charges. The glamour of flying to exotic countries meant that luggage design had to follow. Complete with hangers, this solid suitcase known as the 'Rev-Robe' from the Revelation Suitcase Company was first made in 1928 and reflects the style and allure of the 'jet-set' era.

PHOTOGRAPHY

Introduced in 1888 in New York, the Kodak #1 camera was created by George Eastman (1854–1932), making photography accessible to millions. Taking snapshots became a national craze as families commemorated important events in their lives, such as holidays, weddings and birthdays, and stored them in family albums. Memories were also presented as slides and cine films. The Selo Films envelope here was designed in about 1935–37.

PHOTOGRAPHIC WORK BY

Boots

AGFACOLOR K

Kodak
WALLET

Your photographs.

AGFACOLOR K
20 Diarahmen 24x36

ask for —
'Kodak'
film

SELO FILMS

SELO
SELOCHROME
SELO FINE GRAIN
PANCHROMATIC
SELO HYPERSENSITIVE
PANCHROMATIC

EVERYDAY LABELS
A Dickinson Product

6 GUMMED LABELS
6 TIE-ON LABELS

6 1D 2

MADE IN GREAT BRITAIN
OBLITERATE ALL OLD LABELS ·
SHOW DESTINATION IN BLOCK LETTERS
REF. L.C.P.O.

Kodak

PHOTOGRAPHIC WORK BY

Boots

COSTA BRAVA

Playa de Aro

BOSQUEJO HISTÓRICO

HISTORICAL SKETCH · ESQUISSE HISTORIQUE

TWO GIRLS WROTE HOME FROM PARIS

Joan wrote:

"I suppose I'm enjoying it—but I've got a feeling I might be enjoying it far *more*! You see, no one in the party can speak French properly—and that means delays, mistakes, and an awful feeling of incompetence. We always miss the bus—literally and otherwise! I can't think why I didn't do something about it before we came away!"

Betty wrote:

"Having a marvellous time—and feeling quite like a Parisienne already. It's such fun being able to prattle away in French—and I'm sure it's saving a lot of money! Shopping, sightseeing, sitting in those enchanting cafés—it comes in useful all the time. They've told me that my French is really good, too. Those Linguaphone people did me a good turn."

You can test a Linguaphone Course in any language free! Turn over—and find out how.

LINGUAPHONE for Languages

COURSES IN:

French	Czech
German	Finnish
Spanish	Irish
Portuguese	Afrikaans
Italian	Esperanto
English	Iranian
Dutch	Hindustani
Swedish	Arabic
Russian	Chinese
Polish	Modern Hebrew

Children actually enjoy language study by Linguaphone and learn quickly without strain.

Postage will be paid by Linguaphone Ltd.

No Postage Stamp necessary if posted in Great Britain or Northern Ireland

BUSINESS REPLY CARD
Licence No. 1580

To the Principal,
The LINGUAPHONE Institute,
LINGUAPHONE HOUSE,
207/209, REGENT STREET,
LONDON, W.I.

Norwegian coins---

THEIR VALUES-
AND WHAT THEY
LOOK LIKE

With Compliments of
BERGEN LINE

NORGE I LOMMEFORMAT

Sogn og Fjordane

MALAGA

LA MARCA INTRODUCIDA EN EL MUNDO

GONZALEZ BYASS

FAMOUS THE WORLD OVER
FAMEUSE DANS TOUT LE MONDE

GONZALEZ, BYASS & Co., Ltd.
7/8, Great Winchester Street - LONDON, E. C. 2. (Inglaterra).

2 WAYS TO THE SOUTH

OSLO
FREDERIKSHAVN
KØBENHAVN

D·F·D·S

DET FORENEDE DAMPSKIBS-SELSKAB

For tickets and further information apply to the Travel Bureaux or
JACOB NATVIG & CO.
KARL JOHANSGT. 1, OSLO TLF. 41 71 40, TELEGR.ADR.: JANACO

Oslo Guide

Nr. 9 — 1955

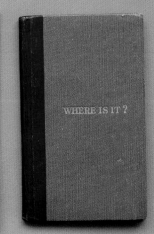

WHERE IS IT?

Hotel
CAMBON

SEVILLA

SEMANA
SANTA

ESPECIALITES - PLATS DE LA REGION
Restaurante *"Pasaje Andaluz"*
SIERPES, 82 Y 84   SEVILLA

3, RUE CAMBON   HOTEL CAMBON - PARIS   Téléphone : Opéra 13-41

3, Rue Cambon   HOT
(près les Tuileries)

GIBRALTAR
and
TANGIER

BEA

TIMETABLE FROM

1 NOVEMBER 1955

BRITISH EUROPEAN AIRWAYS

Issue No. 4

Hotel
Santa Marta

GRANADA

QUERA   134 km.

MALAGA   A. ZIEGLER

ELLA

Midway between Malaga
and Gibraltar ideal for
delightful holidays and for
excursions through
Andalucia or a trip
to Morocco

BEA

FLY BEA IN EUROPE'S
FINEST AIR FLEET

BRITISH EUROPEAN AIRWAYS   VISCOUNT *"Discovery Class"* AEROPLANE.

ESPAÑA
ITINERARIO DE
COSTA BRAVA

Hotel
"Aigua Blava"
PLAYA DE FORNELLS *(Bagur)*
TELEFONO 9 *(Bagur)*

plano-guía

ESPAÑA · SPAIN · ESPAGNE · SPANIEN

BARCELONA

HOTEL PRINCIPE
BARCELONA

NORWAY

KVIKNE HOTEL
BALHOLM

THE IDEAL PLACE
TO SPEND A SUMMER
HOLIDAY

5

TOURIST-MAP
OF
NORWAY

PARADOR

tebravia

POSTCARDS AND GUIDES

In the eighteenth century, Venice attracted merchants and tourists from across Europe and beyond. In search of culture and learning, young aristocrats undertook the Grand Tour, and paintings of Venetian views by artists such as Giovanni Antonio Canal (1697–1768) or Canaletto became extremely popular. Back home, the paintings enabled the Grand Tourists to show their friends and families where they had been. The following century, cheap postage stamps were invented, making mail delivery easy and affordable. Before that, prices for posting letters had been based on the distances postmen had to travel, and recipients rather than senders paid. The new procedure transformed the postal system, and following the same principle as Canaletto's paintings, picture postcards became popular with travellers. The postcards here, from Barcelona, Seville, Norway and Paris, are from the 1950s and 1960s when affordable holidays were in an embryonic stage.

BOOK COVERS

Before the nineteenth century, books were hand-bound in cloth, but in the 1820s, mechanical bookbinding techniques were developed, making books cheaper to produce and easy to print. Techniques for book cover design were borrowed from poster art and graphic design, and book covers evolved into a new art form. As the publishing industry got more competitive, book cover design became more ambitious. These mid-twentieth-century designs were created to attract buyers from crowded shelves, using cheaper methods of printing that were being developed, as well as contemporary trends in type and image.

SHOPPING BAG

BAGS

In the 1850s, Francis Wolle patented a machine he had created to mass-produce paper bags. After that, various paper-bag-making machines were invented to produce different types of paper bags. Often printed with a store's logo or brand colours, many have now become collectable. Here are paper bags from W. H. Smith from 1971 and the 1980s, Harrods from the 1950s and 1980s, a Happy Shopper bag from the 1990s, a bag printed with a *Daily Mail* logo from the 1980s, a D. H. Evans bag from the 1970s and John Lewis bags from before the 1960s.

YVES SAINT LAURENT RIVE GAUCHE

Conceived in 1961 by the Ukrainian-French commercial poster artist Adolphe Mouron Cassandre or Cassandre (1901–68), the Yves Saint Laurent logo was created with a vertical YSL monogram and a horizontal Yves Saint Laurent. Mixing serif and sans serif lettering, and Roman and italic forms, the design broke graphic design conventions. In 1966, the couture house launched its revolutionary first ready-to-wear collection under the name Saint Laurent Rive Gauche with a logo featuring Cassandre's design and orange and pink squares, created by Yves Saint Laurent (1936–2008) in collaboration with the perfume designer Pierre-François Dinand (b.1931).

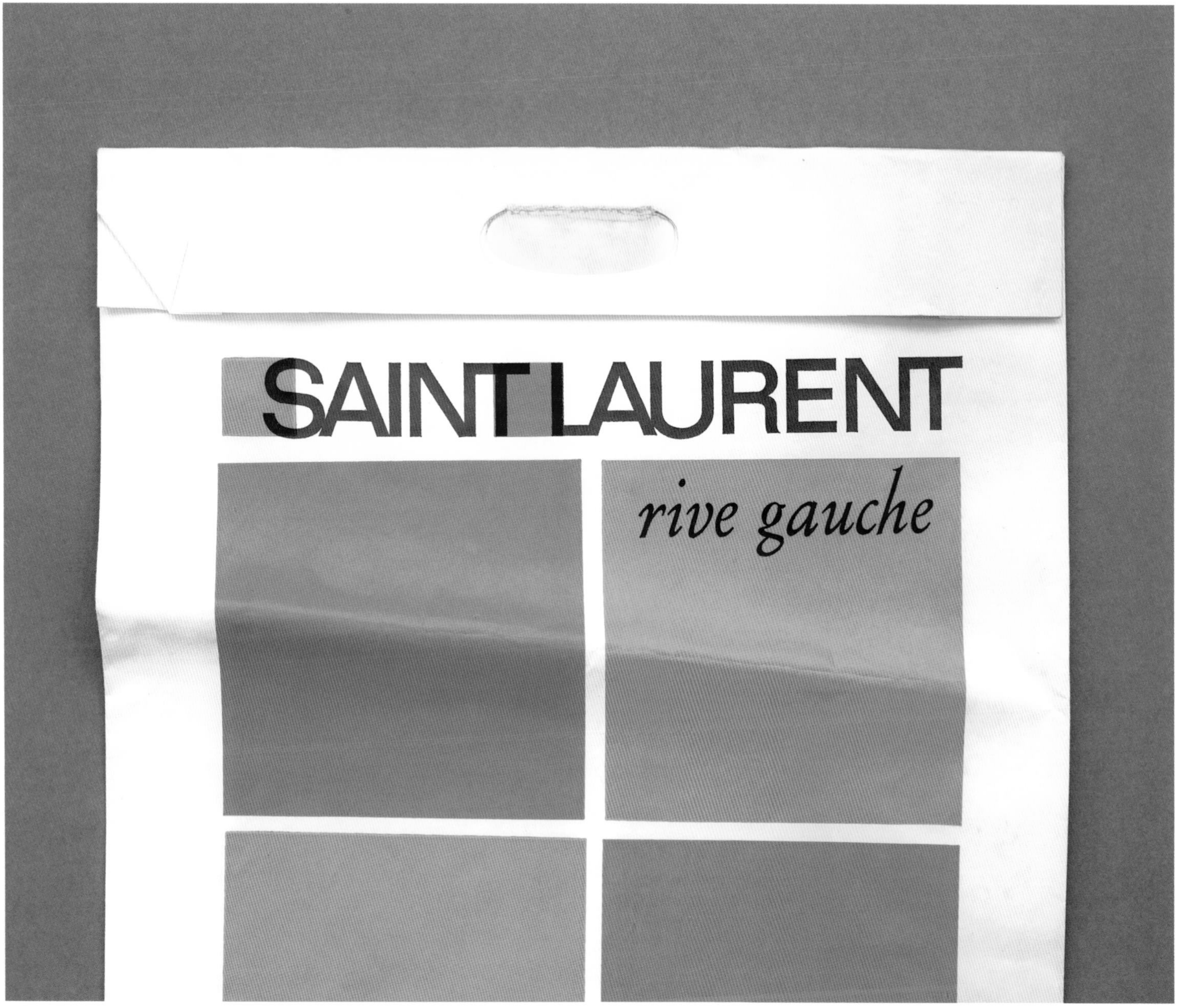
SAINT LAURENT
rive gauche

MAIL ORDER FASHION

The first mail order catalogue was possibly printed in Venice in 1498, advertising books. In 1667, an English gardener published a mail order seed catalogue. In 1744 Benjamin Franklin produced a catalogue of scientific and academic books and in 1861, after the Penny Post had been established and railways extended, the Welsh entrepreneur Pryce Pryce-Jones (1834–1920) produced a mail order catalogue of his wares that he distributed across Britain. It became extremely popular – among his many customers were Florence Nightingale and Queen Victoria. He soon began exporting around the world and, by 1880, he had more than 100,000 customers. The mail order business was established. By the late nineteenth century, almost anything that could be purchased was sold by mail order. Mail order fashion in particular became respectable, particularly among genteel ladies.

SUITS

Garment	Style Number	Tweed or Flannel Number	Garment	Style Number	Tweed or Flannel Number
SUIT JACKET			TOPS		
SUIT SKIRT			WAISTCOATS		

| Bust | Waist | Hips | Skirt length from top of waistband | | |

REMARKS: Any information you can give about your figure, i.e. long or short waisted, unusually thin, thick, short or long arm, broad shoulder width, prominent bust, hips, seat or thighs will be helpful.

top tailoring for boys

Mid-grey suits with trousers or shorts

'Popular' grade wool flannel suits, reinforced with 10% nylon to give extra hard wear and long-lasting good looks.
Suits with trousers. BRD635. 1, sizes 7-8 **£9.** 9-10 **10.0.** 11-12 **£12.12.6.**
Suits with shorts. BRD555-1, sizes 7-8 **94.6.** 2-3 **99.6.** 4-5 **£5.7.6.** 6-8 **£5.15.0.**
Trousers to match suit above. BRD555-1. sizes 7-8 **66.-** 9-10 **68.-** 11-12 **76.-**
Shorts with double seats to match above suit. Sizes 1 **29.6.** 2-3 **31.9.** 6-8 **35.9.**
These same good looking suits are also available in pure worsted.
Suits with trousers from **£11.5.0** to **£13.10.0.**
Suits with shorts from **£6.5.6** to **£7.10.0.**

Navy blazers

'Collegiate' quality in a handsome and hard-wearing wool cloth with nylon added for extra strength. Single-breasted style with lined sleeves. BRD102, chest 24 **60.-;** 26 **62.-;** 28-30 **67.6;** 32 **76.-;** 34 **80.-.**

Navy gaberdine raincoats

'Collegiate' grade—top quality gaberdine and linings tailored into the best school raincoats you will see anywhere. Lined throughout with additional protection at vulnerable points and proofed to stand up to all but the very worst weather. BRD378, lengths 26" **£6.16.8.** rising 5— each 2" size to 42" **£6.19.0.** then 44" **£9.**
'Popular' grade, well tailored from a fine quality navy union gaberdine at an economical price. BRD377, lengths 26" **97.6.** rising 5— each 2" size to 42" **£6.17.6.** then 44" **£7.7.6.**

navy blazers and raincoats for girls

In our girls department are navy blazers and navy gaberdine raincoats, tailored in girls' sizes and proportions by the same people who make these leading clothes for boys. Sizes and prices are similar to those given above.

Eton collar sweater (left) in heavy-knit pure wool. Cream, grey or navy-blue. BYS38, chest 30 **42.6;** 32 **44.-;** 34 **45.6;** 34" **51.6;** 36" **55.6.**

V-neck games sweater (left, below), heavy-knit in all wool. Cream only. BYS31, chest 30 **36.-;** 32 **37.-;** 34 **40.-;** 34" **47.6;** 36" **50.6.**

Cream flannels (not illus.)—shorts and trousers in a good quality wool cotton mixture which washes and wears well. Trousers: BRD585, sizes 7-8 **62.-;** 9-10 **66.-;** 11-12 **72.-.**
Shorts: BRD419, sizes 3-5 **36.-;** 6-8 **38.-.**

Inexpensive ripple-knit cotton cardigan (below, left) with easy raglan sleeves and two pockets. SGL284, chest 26" **16.0;** 30" **17.6;** 32" 36" **19.6.**

Ribbed cotton knit jumper (left) in white, with cap sleeves for complete freedom of movement. SGL101, sizes 28 —36 **9.6.**

[Shoes, right column]

433 Laced-to-toe tennis shoes by Dunlop in white ventilex canvas with sponge insole and crepe outsole. Boys' sizes 2-5 **17.6;** 6-12 **21.6.**

458 Running shoes made by experts with experts in mind. Supple, black leather uppers with strong flexible leather soles and screw spikes. Normal fitting, sizes 6-10. **47.6.**

442 Cricket shoes with finely studded leather soles and heels, in white or brown canvas. Normal fitting, sizes 1-5. **42.9;** 6-10 **46.9.**

446 Cricket boots in durable white canvas lined with leather. Stout leather soles and heels, well studded, giving a firm grip. Normal fitting, sizes 1-5. **48.9;** 6-10 **52.9.**

Almost the Star of the collection. An infinitely desirable suit, tailored for town or country living, in wonderful camel. Jacket has side vents, flapped pockets and leather buttons. Skirt is perfectly slim with Dior pleat at back. See how sportily it mates with Polo Neck pullover (available in camel shade only). This pullover comes with our new "travelling sleeve"—so called because it travels up or down the arm. Special double-ribbed cuff keeps it smartly in position—whether worn down to the wrist, or up as three-quarter length sleeve.
Suit 751/728. Price £28 17s. 6d.
Pullover PS/D/78. Price £5 5s. 6d.

As soft and as straight as you can go. A slimline camel skirt fully lined with invisible zip, and Dior pleat at back. Happily married to chic cardigan with attractive tailored collar. Special ribbing prevents stretch . . . holds that fresh, crisp look. Our new "travelling sleeves" are here again, and can be worn long or three-quarter length.
Skirt 729. Price £9 19s. 6d.
Cardigan PS/D/74. Price £6 12s. 6d.

Don't try and live without this marvellous, adaptable waistcoat. Single-breasted, with large covered buttons and two pockets. Darts behind give an easy blouse effect. Slim-line skirt and long-sleeved blouse get together and make this one of your smartest most livable-in outfits. Well—you can see how gorgeous it looks!
Waistcoat 710. Price £4 19s. 6d. **Skirt 3050.** Price £5 5s. 6d.
Shirt 643 Price £3 19s. 6d.
THIS WAISTCOAT SHOULD BE ORDERED ON THE 'SUITS' PAGE OF THE ORDER BOOK

page 14   page 15

Hogskin Gloves PS/16. Price £3.12.6.   **Silk Scarf PS/12.** Price £2.12.6.

I call them "super-gloves" and it's hard to think of a better name. They just do have that super-quality feel about them . . . so soft, elegant, flexible. AND they're made-to-measure. (Surprising what a difference that makes.) Not only do they look much better, but they wear much longer. That's important to all of us! In Oatmeal or Mushroom shades. Measure as for Lambskin Gloves.

These scarves are easily the most . . . well, all I can say is that they are easily the most *everything!* The most bright. The most gay. The most fun. The most deliriously lovely. They are newly designed for me by Richard Allen in pure silk (twill) and I've never known anything to do more for tweeds and flannels. Something about them that highlights the colours and makes a whole outfit *sing*. They come in two-tone shades that blend with all your Peter Saunders' clothes. And I'm so sure you'll be enchanted with them—I'm even ready to send you one on approval!

Let's talk SUITS

Know what I feel about fashion! I feel it should be more of a *game*. A game of colours and styles and ideas that you can play with yourself. And perhaps this, more than anything, is the inspiration behind the Peter Saunders' suit collection.

Look on, and see what fun you can have. For with Peter Saunders, you can be your own designer. In fact, it's a game where you hold all the trumps—for all the materials are so perfectly colour-matched, you *cannot* go wrong. You can mix and mingle to your heart's content: tweeds and flannels, plain and check designs, light colours, dark colours . . . it goes on for ever. And every way is right and beautiful.

It's YOUR personality that counts

This is an age of mass production and chain stores; and Peter Saunders is one of the few *individual* services left: one of the few ways to express your taste, your personality in clothes—instead of just wearing what thousands of other women wear. All our tweeds are woven from special, high-twist yarn. This ensures that your suit will resist crushing, need remarkably little pressing, and wear endlessly. As one customer said: "Your tweed suits are the female equivalent of my husband's thorn-proof jackets!"

In this era of 'mass production' all our coats and suits are tailored (and hand-tailored!) the same way as they were in

---

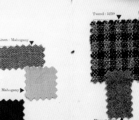

Knitwear: Mahogany
Tweed : 5259   Tweed : 5259
Linen : Mahogany
Poplin : Mahogany
Flannel 20/45   Worsted Terylene : Mahogany   Flannel 20 56

HARRODS

One of the world's largest and most famous department stores, Harrods in London's Knightsbridge covers over a million square feet (90,000 square metres). Known for selling luxury and everyday items across seven floors and in 330 departments, its motto is *Omnia Omnibus Ubique* – All Things for All People, Everywhere. Established in 1849 by Charles Henry Harrod, the store began in a single room, selling tea and groceries and employing just two assistants and a messenger boy. By 1880, it was a flourishing department store, selling a wide range of goods and attracting wealthy customers. After a fire in 1883, the store was rebuilt with a distinctive terracotta-clad Art Nouveau and Baroque frontage. The store became a public company in 1889 and in 1898 it added one of the world's first escalators. Its prestigious reputation has endured.

HARRODS

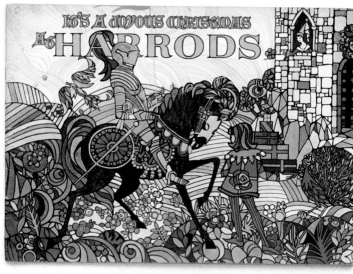

IT'S A JOYOUS CHRISTMAS
AT HARRODS

Harrods
Magical
Christmas

Harrods
ENCHANTED CHRISTMAS
1968

Harrods
PRESENT

CHRISTMAS IN WONDERLAND   1969

Come to
Harrods
The Land of Father Christmas

The Voyage o
YOUR COMFORT
Harrods is the Land of
We have turned the w
wonderful Christmas a
unique and special fa
HARRODS LTD   KNI

HABERDASHERY AND TOOL BOX

SEWING

The twentieth century was less of a throwaway period than the early twenty-first; if socks or stockings were damaged, they were repaired. Buttons, hooks and eyes and press studs were replaced when missing or broken, and sewing tasks were usually undertaken by women, who kept a fully-stocked needlework basket or box in the home. During World War Two, 'Make Do and Mend' emphasized renewing and mending clothes and soft furnishings. There were sewing and knitting circles ('Knitting or Sewing for Victory') and this was a common use of spare time, either for friends and family or to send to the armed forces, and so the work basket was imperative.

EMBROIDERY THREADS

In approximately 1800, two cousins, Jonathan (1783–1869) and William (1782–1829) Harris opened a weaving shop in Cockermouth, Cumbria, where flax had been grown for centuries. The shop's success enabled them to buy the Low Gote Mill nearby in around 1808, and in 1834, the Derwent Mill as well. Although at first their mills were powered by water, steam engines were installed in 1835 and 1849. By the 1850s, the Harris family supplemented its original business of flax preparation, yarn-spinning and weaving with the additional production of sewing threads, substituting linen for silk. They had discovered that the flax fibre could retain almost all colours that are used on other fibres such as silk, wool and cotton, and Harris flax embroidery threads became used widely, including for the finest embroidery that would usually have been created with silk thread. Despite the firm's long and successful history, it closed during the Great Depression in 1934.

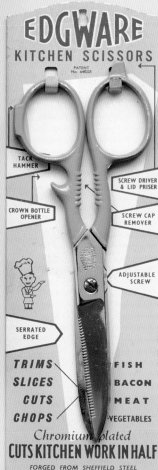
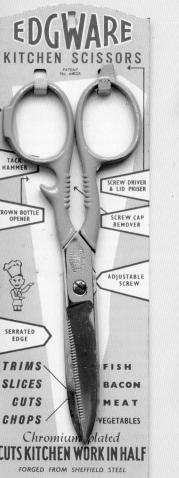

TOOLS

In the early 1960s, Greensleeves produced 'quality garden tools.' These secateurs were made in 1961. The small blue plastic policeman-shaped Ingersoll Lok-eeze bottle contains powdered graphite, which was squeezed into a lock that needed easing, and in the 1950s before domestic central heating was widespread, the Tombac Draught Sealing Strip was helpful for draughty homes.

AMMUNITION

Winchester Ammunition manufactures ammunition for all shooting activities, including hunting, shooting at targets and for personal defence. This box of Winchester cartridges dates from 1914.

MILBRO
"CALEDONIAN"
·22 WAISTED SLUGS
No. 2 Bore - 5½ m.m.
NOMINAL 250
MADE IN ENGLAND

BRITISH MADE
"WASP"
(REG'D)
500
PELLETS
No. 1 (·177)
AIR RIFLES
Manufactured at the
Kynoch Factories of Imperial Chemical
Industries Limited, Metals Division
Witton, Birmingham, England

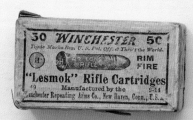

50 WINCHESTER 50
Trade Marks Reg. U. S. Pat. Off. & Thro' the World.
.22 LONG RIFLE
RIM
FIRE
"Lesmok" Rifle Cartridges
Manufactured by the
Winchester Repeating Arms Co., New Haven, Conn., U.S.A.

Webley
AIR RIFLES · AIR PISTOLS · SPORTING GUNS · ETC
APPROX. 500
·22 SPECIAL WAISTED PELLETS

TOY CHEST AND ATTIC

PUPPET

One of the great names of British toy manufacturing, Pelham Puppets was started by ex-serviceman Bob Pelham (1919–80) after World War Two in 1947. The company remained in business until 1993. Initially called Wonky Toys Ltd after Bob's nickname, it produced simple wooden toys held together with string. Within a few years, Bob began making marionettes for children as until then, these were made only for adult, professional use. They were enormously successful and during the company's lifetime, over 500 different characters were created, from horses to witches, farmers to fairies, housewives to clowns. In 1953, the company secured the right to manufacture Disney characters, and of those they produced Pinocchio was the most popular. This Baby Dragon was first manufactured in c.1961.

GAMES

Indoor games have been played for thousands of years, but were particularly developed during the Victorian era, and by the 1950s and 1960s, emerged as a way families bonded in the home. Board and card games blend the elements of chance, skill and rivalry. Descending from ancient Egypt and claiming to have been played during the Trojan War, draughts – or checkers – is a board game of strategy. Card game classics such as Snap and Happy Families retain their appeal, especially at family gatherings, and Lego, founded in 1932 by Ole Kirk Kristiansen (1891–1958), has continued to evolve into a worldwide phenomenon. In the sixteenth century, a lottery game was invented in Italy. By the 1880s and 1890s, it had become known as Lotto across Europe and Bingo in the US. It was popular as a boxed game. Early manufacturers in Britain included Spears, Waddingtons, Parker Brothers and J. Harris.

WOODLAND
Happy Families
CARD GAME

5 4

PICTURED BY
RACEY HELPS

Happy
Families

CHAD VALLEY

7 c In the Land of the Giants

A Visit to the Queen
The Marrow Bone
Fighting the Wasps
The Giant Finger

GULLIVER'S TRAVELS
No 293
THE STORY IS TOLD ON THE
BACKS OF THE CARDS
PIATNIK – VIENNA
BENNO PRODUCTS LONDON
Made in Austria

ROUND THE WORLD
CARD GAME

Pepys

3
Austral

LEGO
The Building Toy

431

THE
CROWN DRAUGHT
BRITISH MADE

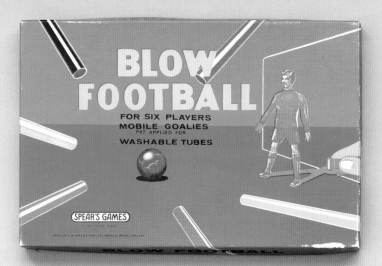

BLOW FOOTBALL

FOR SIX PLAYERS
MOBILE GOALIES
PAT APPLIED FOR
WASHABLE TUBES

SPEAR'S GAMES

DRESS UP
SNAP

PLAYING
Card

9		20	30	£		
2	16		46		-70	84
	27	38			71	86
			51	66		

76

52

43

Dressing Up

**Made in England
by-
Dressing Up
London N.W.I.**

LOTTO
OR HOUSEY - HOUSEY

MADE IN ENGLAND

TARGET GAMES

for any number of players (7 years upwards)

I.C.A.

WADDINGTON'S game of
JACK
STRAWS

PULL-ALONG DOG

After World War Two, Britain struggled through years of
financial hardship. Reductions were made in many areas,
including in manufacture, construction and materials.
Rationing continued for several goods, including petrol
and some foods, beyond 1945, but even after the last
rationing ended in 1954, many areas of production
remained depressed. Toys were one group of items that
in general were produced as cheaply as possible. Doll's
house furniture, toy weapons, dolls and some pull-along
animals such as this red sausage dog made in the late
1950s, were made of brightly coloured, heat-moulded,
exceptionally thin, hollow plastic.

CUDDLY TOYS AND BABY STROLLER

After World War One, brothers Walter, William and Arthur Lines named their new toy-manufacturing company Tri-Ang, as triangles are made of three lines. By 1947, Tri-Ang claimed to be the largest toy company in the world, and it continued until 1971. The brothers' father was Joseph Lines, who ran the wooden toy making company G & J Lines (1876–1930) with his carpenter brother George.

Teddy bears have comforted young children and babies since the early twentieth century and many have become collectables. Different manufacturers created various stylistic elements, such as longer or shorter arms or snouts and dumpy or slim bodies.

ARTS AND CRAFTS

Long before laptops, tablets and mobile phones, when television programmes were fairly limited, crafts featured highly in many households, particularly occupying children. Before and after World War Two, gummed paper squares, alphabet or animal stencils were often used for decorating scrapbooks, and many eleven year olds, embarking on their first term at senior school, were presented with a box of mathematical instruments, comprising compasses, a ruler, set squares and protractors.

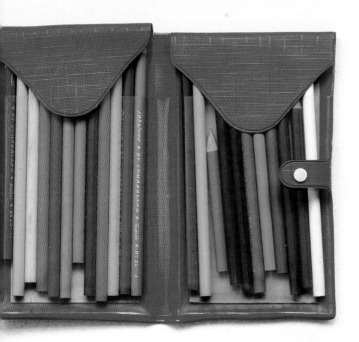

Granville Gummed Chain Papers

REEVES
"PUTTY" RUBBER
for use with chalk or charcoal drawings

L & C HARDTMUTH (GREAT BRITAIN) LTD
KOH-I-NOOR
ONE DOZEN
KOH-I-NOOR
PENCILS
BRITISH MADE

LEMON YELLOW

ONE GROSS
Coloured
DRAWING PINS
STOCKED IN SIX COLOURS AS SHOWN
BRITISH MADE   WHITE

The Modern Students
set of Mathematical Instruments
MADE IN ENGLAND

Jollycraft
ALPHABET
STENCIL
SET
Complete with numerals
Made and Printed in Great Britain,
Wiggins Teape (Stationery) Limited

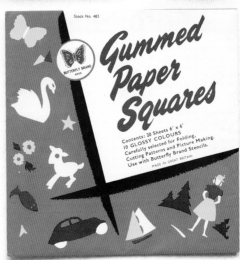
Stock No. 483
BUTTERFLY BRAND
Gummed
Paper
Squares
Contents: 20 Sheets 6" x 6"
10 GLOSSY COLOURS
Carefully selected for Folding,
Cutting Patterns and Picture Making.
Use with Butterfly Brand Stencils.
MADE IN GREAT BRITAIN

25mm x 33m
(Replaces 1" x 36 Yds)
Sellotape
self-adhesive tape

Sellotape
REGD TRADE MARK
self-adhesive
clear tape

THE FANTASTIC WORLD OF **CORGI**TOYS

Bandolero
4½ ins. 41-1. Price 45p.

Mercedes C.111
4 ins. 44-1. Price 45p.

56

...sleek European G.T's for speed and luxury

Always something new from
DINKY TOYS

No.5
3'

IB

Britains Models
MODELS MARKED "NEW ADDITION" AVAILABLE FROM APRIL/MAY

6ᴰ 1969

MATCHBOX
COLLECTORS CATALOGUE-1973-5p

57

MATCHBOX

IB Zoo MODELS

1351 Large Camel 1'8
1352 Baby Camel 1'2
1354 American Bison 2'9
1356 Water Buffalo 1'4

1357 Zebra 1'4
1358 Eland 1'4
1359 Antelope 10d
1360 Wild Boar 10d
1361 Anteater 10d
1362 Tapir

1364 Red Deer 10d
1366 Llama 10d
1368 Springbuck 8d
1369 Wolf 8d
1370 Large Kangaroo 10d
1371

ADD BRITAINS TREE MODELS TO YOUR ZOO
Bring your Zoo to life. Use ribbons to make up models. See Page 28.

1311 Indian Elephant 4'11
(6.2 cms. high)
1313 Baby Elephant 1'2

Nissan Elephant

1326 Young Crocodile 1'8

Bertone Runabout
(with opening engine compartment)
K-31
Price 45p

a police car ready to pounce . . .

57

super toy models 1975

B REGD TRADE MARK

BRITAINS

BRITAINS

SUPER

TOYS

1971

2½p 6ᴰ

©1971 BRITAINS LIMITED

B

Britains Toy Models 1970 6ᴰ

Always something new from

DINKY TOYS

No6
3ᴰ

TOY CATALOGUES

Corgi cars were first made in 1956 by Mettoy Playcraft Ltd. The first item was a wind-up car made with a cast aluminium body and tin plate wheels. The earliest Corgi cars, made in die-cast zinc, included a Ford Consul, an Austin A50 Cambridge, a Morris Cowley, an Austin-Healey 100 and a Triumph TR2, but the company became famous for its more exciting cars, particularly the Batmobile and Bond cars, with such additions as ejector seats, suspension, opening doors, bonnets and boots, and sparkling headlights.

Dinky Toys were first made in Liverpool, England in 1934 as a by-product of Hornby railway sets. Within a year, over one hundred models had been created. Dinky, whose models were smaller than Corgi's, also produced models of aircraft, ships and military vehicles as well as cars and lorries, but in the end, the brand lost popularity and stopped manufacturing in 1979.

TOYS

Dolls are the earliest-known toy figures, with archaeological evidence of some made of clay, stone, wood, bone and ivory. Some have been found in Egyptian tombs from the twenty-first century BC and dolls with movable limbs have been discovered in Greece from approximately 200 BC. Mechanical or wind up figures became particularly popular during the 1950s and 1960s, evolving from tin to plastic. Among these wind-up figures are a Donald Duck made by TOMY in the 1970s, a Pac-Man Blue Ghost also made by TOMY in 1982 and a Cubby Bear from the 1950s, made in Japan by ALPS.

CHRISTMAS

After Prince Albert introduced the Christmas tree to England in the 1840s, decorations for the home became more widespread and elaborate. Initially, during the Victorian and Edwardian eras, many were expensive, but gradually, a range of decorations were produced to suit all pockets. From the 1920s and throughout World War Two, paper and card decorations were popular, paper chains and lanterns adorned living rooms and glass and tin items were hung on Christmas trees. In the 1950s and 1960s, plastic and nylon took greater prominence.

CANDLE HOLDER

Before World War Two, most candle chimes were made in Germany of lithographed polished tin, often embossed and with several moving parts. Throughout World War Two and for a number of years beyond, the manufacture of these ornaments stopped. In their place, Danish, Swedish and other northern European manufacturers began producing candle chimes. Although they resembled the German versions, they were less complex and elaborate and usually made with plain, flat brass, rather than embossed, lithographed tin. This Avebe Swedish-made angel chime was a popular Christmas decoration in Europe and North America throughout the second half of the twentieth century and into the twenty-first. When the four small candles are lit, the heat creates an updraught of air that in turn forces the horizontal wheel to rotate, which then turns the angels.

WRAPPING

The earliest use of wrapping paper was almost certainly in ancient China, where paper was invented in the second century BC. During the Song Dynasty, rulers gave government officials gifts of money wrapped in paper envelopes. So gift wrapping had been invented for centuries already when Joyce Clyde Hall (1891–1982) and his older brothers Rollie (1888–1961) and Bill (dates unknown) helped to popularize the idea of decorative gift wrapping after they ran out of the tissue paper they used to wrap gifts in at their stationery shop (Hallmark) in Kansas City, Missouri. Rollie found some fancy French paper they had intended to use to line envelopes and sold it instead at 10 cents a sheet. It sold out. The following year, the brothers repeated the sale of the fancy French paper, and again, it sold out rapidly. Soon, the brothers began printing their own special wrapping paper, which encouraged a new industry.

CHRISTMAS MODELS

Decorating cakes with marzipan (or 'marchpane') and sugared piping began in Europe during the sixteenth century, although it is possible that some ancient peoples also decorated their own sweetmeats. Decorating cakes with dainty trinkets developed in Europe in the seventeenth century. Rich fruit, iced wedding and Christmas cakes were especially adorned with novelties during the Victorian era, only halted in World War Two and have continued ever since. These little figurines date from the 1970s and 80s.

ACKNOWLEDGEMENTS

It was Polly Powell who saw inside Granny's kitchen cupboard and first proposed this book.

My thanks to Susie Hodge for her hard work on the background and history of the cupboard's contents. At Pavilion Books, Bella Cockrell has been an editor of unfailing efficiency and enthusiasm. Thank you too to publishing director Katie Cowan.

For the look and layout, credit goes to design manager Laura Russell, designer James Boast and photographer Tony Briscoe and his team.

Caroline Porter is at the heart of the book. Her photographs inspired it in the beginning and her support throughout has made it what it is.

If there are errors in this book, they are mine alone.

REFERENCES

Lewis, John. *Collecting Printed Ephemera: a background to social habits and social history, to eating and drinking, to travel and heritage* (1976). London: Studio Vista.

Martin, Kathy. *Famous Brand Names and Their Origins* (2017). Barnsley: Pen and Sword Books.

Miller, Judith. *Miller's 20th Century Design* (2012). London: Octopus Books.

Tambini, Michael. Consultants: Robert Opie and Professor Jonathan M. Woodham. *The Look of the Century: Design Icons of the 20th Century* (1999). London: Dorling Kindersley.

Image on page 6 ©Imperial War Museum (A 25726)

INDEX

Page references in *italics* refer to illustrations

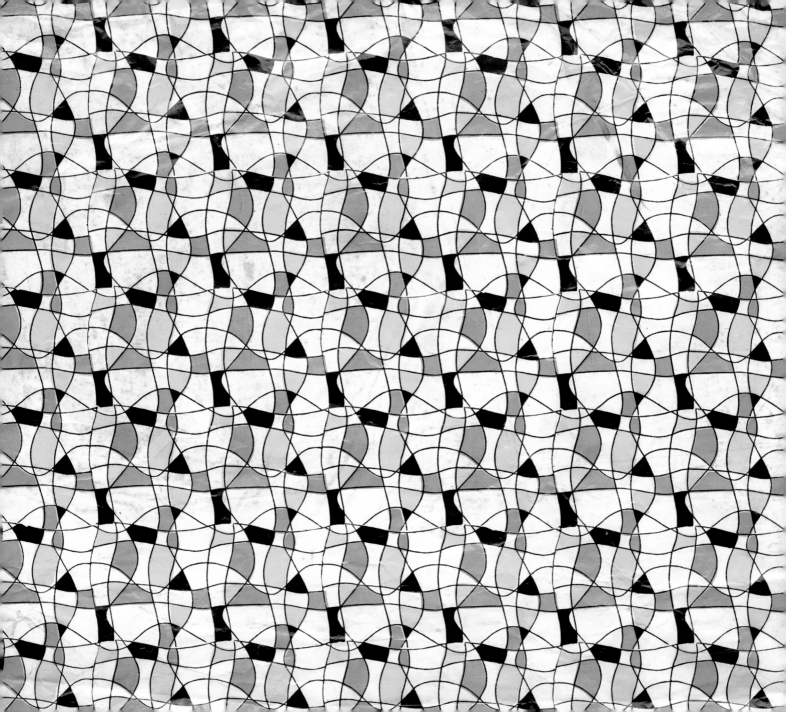